enter light – exit light
and everything in between

A Boomer's Life in Poems

Gary Johnson

enter light – exit light and everything in between

Johnson Publishing
2002 Vandorf Road
Aurora, Ontario
L4G 7B9

First Printing, 2017

Cover Image by Gary Johnson
Cover & Interior Design by Infinite Pathways Press

10 9 8 7 6 5 4 3 2 1

For my wife Cathy and the Cleveland Hill Gang

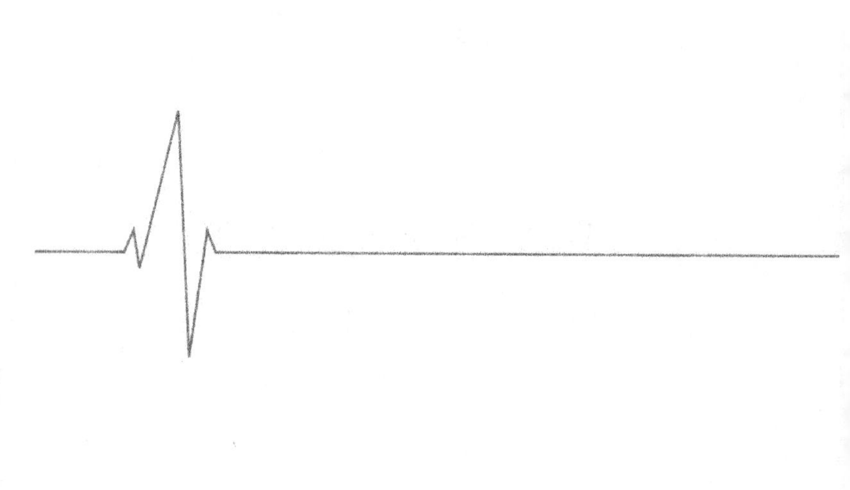

enter light –

Sleep's Sunrise

Dark well-hole blackness
to warm dawn orange,
and light blurs through lashes
till my eyes focus and open.

Mind Gyre

Ether eyes in the beach sand,
Body between the water and sky,
Neither up nor down,
But one to two,
Rushing the horizon,
Blue and blue and blue;

Finally flying toward the searing sun,
Faster and higher and higher,
Hoping my climb will never end,
But I've reached my acme
because the wings that Icarus gave me
are beginning to melt and burn;
And I am falling free,
slower and lower and lower
in large sweeping circles
I drift apart the heaven of stars
with singular silence,
through clouds that mark the graves
of dead harpies,
and the gods of man are all there,
from Apollo to Amen Ra,
and Zeus to Allah,

and witness the dry decay
of the ruins of the tower of Babel
where man tried to meet them half-way;
And as I slowly descend
into the lower levels of heaven,
I hear the echo of ack ack
and see the skeletons and smoke
of planes from world wars;
and I am in the sea.

Ballerina

She never got her way
until her body
gave her favours
and she let
little school boy brothers
and old distant fathers
take her in cinder lanes
and soggy veranda couches.

She dreamed of being a ballerina.

Sequel

on the roof he stands
in the open
a spectre from the past
with rifle raised
above his banded head
a wounded knee spirit
full and flaunting
that cannot be captured
or deadened – now
by soldiers hidden
beyond a frontier curtain

Rhyme without reason

Driven into experienced hands
of older women
Who welcome the hard organs
of younger men
By confirmed virgins
who pine and pant
For some distant husband
who in the end
Doesn't want
an unbroken hymen.

Patron of the Arts

At the door of the penthouse castle
she led us into her never-seen museum,
And we sat among
her horde
of painter's eyes
and sculptor's hands
while she read our letter.

Only then in waiting silence
did we realize her answer.

In moneyed isolation
she feeds from other lives
through the artistic connection,
trying to share
their love and sweat,
through these pieces
they've become her personal slaves

What's in an idea.

A Venus of flesh and fancy

From the dark purple shadows
into the soft humid light,
From the narrow crowded woods
into the wide free lea,
An image of white and brown
walked a path
Through the water fountain,
A slow sensual stride,
that gave my mind and penis a ride,

To where
         A face of faultless form
is to be kissed every inch and corner,
And beautiful, bountiful breasts
that were meant to be cupped with hands
And suckled with lips and tongue,
And between her warm therm thighs
And deeper beyond the golden down,
A man comes
where he began
his origin,
through the ritual of joy
and of great wonder
to maybe start another
small girl-loving boy.

The dream ends, out of her sight,
And I know, I'll never have that night,
but now,
for all time,
she is my fanciful fantasy,
sexual and sensual,
symbol of love.

The Stage for Violence

In the country,
There is softness
That fills and soothes
The eyes,
With colours
Of green trees,
Brown earth,
And blue skies.

In the country,
There is peace
That caresses the neck
And gentles to sleep.
The only sounds
Chew the cud
And suck the udder,
As they look on.

In the country,
There is greatness
That makes man, God.
For when he looks
Over and up,

Nothing will dwarf him
Except his own thoughts
Of nature's façade.

In the country,
There is peace
After the storms
That fills no eyes,
With colours
Of brown skies,
Blue earth,
And the trees...

In the glass

Looking behind,
down the street,
All is empty,
except the figure
of a girl.

Store stopping,
window waiting,

she appears in the glass,
and I stand there,
unaware of the knickknacks
on display.

She moves on,
to another show.
I hesitate
and then follow.

I appear in the glass
and she stands there.

I say hello.
She starts,
and makes to run away,
but I tell her
I won't hurt her,
and she stays.

We appear in the glass,
and we stand there, aware.

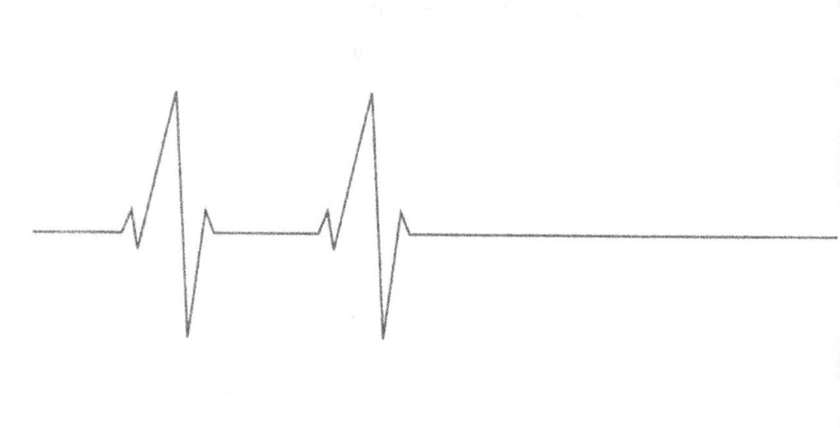

Out of sync

In terms
of words and pictures,
our love and events
were in different lights.

My inner blindness
saw unpleasant household images
that I couldn't talk about,
and you couldn't see.

In your death
you will appear
in the corners
of my eyes,
and I will swear
you are there.

In my death,
you will never
be able
to conjure me.

We have trouble
understanding each other.

The Taming Game of Jane's

The Jane-dream drifts
across the sea-shore horizon
in rich-red shadows
of deep dusk.

A dream?
    But she is there
    for real and rare,
    leaving the dark mist
    waiting to be kissed.

She is the girl
    With
        Long straw-blonde hair
    And
        Flashing blue-eyes,
    Who
        Wears sweaters
    And
        Blue jeans well.

She is the child
    Who
        Turns her head
    And
        Greets you
    With
        A quick smile.

She is the woman
    Who
        Suggestively flirts
    And
        Laughs easily
    Who
        Says she is ugly
    But
        Knows better
    Because
        She has the secret.....

She makes men love her.

the picture

a man and a camera
looking for an ideal image
with the right light
abstraction and juxtaposition
colours and framing
in the mundane or the exotic
where it all comes together
and interlocks with a click
in that quintessential
moment in time

Dundas & Yonge circa 1968

Nicotine stained-glass windows
And absorbed odors of hops,
Drunk gnawing sidewalk crack,
Triple feature Grade B's in neons.
Step by spit on ground.

Rock pounding smoggy air,
Four-lane traffic in slow procession,
A fuzz of cops hand-waving between street
cars,
Horns and lights and exhaust,
Buildings corroded from 50 years of living.

Bums and broads cheap,
1930 suits second-hand from crippled
civilian,
Tight, tight sweater and skirt padded,
Slink, shuffle, wiggle, stumble,
Hunches and curves walking up and down.

Dundas & Yonge is false, cruel and hard,
As is life.

Scythian Storm

Oh, Lady Hurricane,
I sense your passion
beneath
your calm centres
and strands of storm,

While,
breathing in sucks
of love's heavy fragrance,

She conducts
magnetic static current
that holds and touches
in a hair ruffle
and shirt ripple, embrace.

And leaves like last night's whore
after the loving stroke,

To return
In a black, shriek temper,

She appears as a one-breasted Amazon
and tears at your clothes,
and rants and raves her rape,
swiping your face with the back of the hand
sky,
aiming earth's casual arrows
at a body
you once called yours.

Moth of four wool eyes

We met
between county towns
along the washboard road.

The late light
and early night,

Led us to try
to find
some place to stay.

Across fallow fields
into an empty farmyard
stands a weather-beaten barn.

She takes the loft,
and I take the stall.

In the hay,
there is a straining torment
of only a few feet away.

I call her name,
but it comes out in a whisper
that she takes for imagination.
And I repeat it, only louder,
Are you asleep?
or should we keep, our honour.

A mysterious moth
flutters into her chamber.
She yells for help
and I put it away forever.

She nodded her thanks
with which, began her surrender,
in embrace, down to the ground,
we are now, totally together.

More or less than vision

Eyes,
with a wink suggest
or half-hooded to disguise
or closed-tight in disgust,
and wide with surprise.

Eyes,
in frenetic fun,
that roll like Eddie Cantor's,
and go up and down,
and move to cross over.

Eyes,
that look up in thought,
that look down in distress
that look away to avert
exposing the depth of our essence.

But can eyes love,
and kiss and touch?
Can eyes hold hands,
and lay upon a couch?

Eyes express,
But bodies possess.

Hangover From Death

Life and death caught up with me
With her in the climax of the love course,
Heated throbbing satisfaction became
Cold rigid loss.

Sounds, sights, smells, tastes and touch
Of my span exploded in one flash.
A silent, unmoving hypnotic daydream,
Shadowed faces cross the plane of stippled
ceiling,
Black suits to black cars to black earth.

Mumbling minister wastes words,
Sniffing unknowns among the bowed
heads,
Let me be quiet in the grave,
Hurry, tuck in my earth patch.

The wind wipes my tombstone,
A derby wreath my pillow,
The sky my television,
Frozen earth my cake,
Near-by blunt shovels, my life dramas.

At first, weekly visits, her and many others,
Then yearly visits, her and him,
Then none, no one.

A.W.O.L.

absorbed in a book
my love left me
in the epilogue
never to be seen again…….

addicted to a sport
my love left me
in the overtime
never to be seen again…….

asleep on the beach
my love left me
in the undertow
never to be seen again…….

La música muchachos

His father was a mariachi man
who strummed the streets
and sang in cantinas
while passing the hat
to reluctant touristas
and he never had to turn pages
to find music to play.

In the open doorway of his room
the light shines on his intensity
as he woodenly bows his violin
where older brothers left from
to make their fortune
performing in the national orchestra.

They, too, learned from the foreign man.

The awe of our fates

You were there.
a being, I was never able to realize.
across an ocean,
yet we lived and came to be in the same
age,
and you are of my time.

It was your decision,
your courage and mind,
to or not to
sail the sea here,
another land.

The odds were still enormous
or not even there,
but the fates found you this house,
and I easily found your stair.

We might have been the "two ships that
pass in the night",
but the lines of our lives did meet,
and we are together,

in the touch of our hands,
in the sight of our eyes,
in the memory of our minds.

It's something,
nothing and no one can erase,
it's our own history,
and now that can never change.

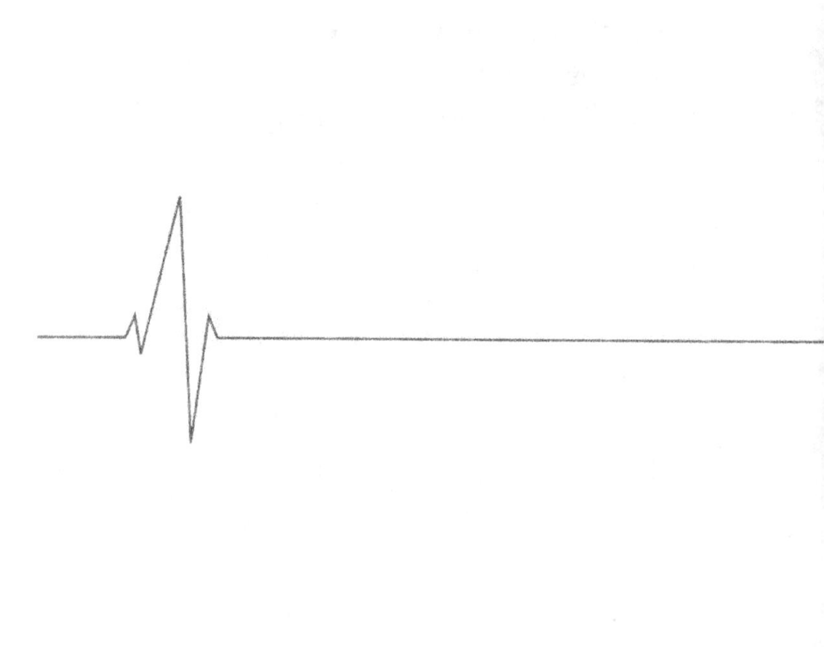

Time ago

for you,
old railroader
though
your pocket watch
still keeps time
though
your pot belly stove
still shines
those whistles
became distant whistles
and no trains
stop in your station
anymore

Seven visions of Lynda

Her name is Lynda,
A word of simple Spanish,
beautiful bella-Lynda,
They would approve for she is.

Black hair,
that seeks the breeze
and she doesn't care.

Warm is the heat
of blush
in her cheeks
that compliments
the blues
of her eyes.

She shapes the couch
with her willowy body
in easy slouch
that would arouse
the animal
in any male.

She sometimes hates,
or acts
tough and hard,

But her true traits
come unarmed
as the madonnic mother,
when she holds Christopher
in her arms.

And when,
she enters,
and you see her;
You wish,
that she,
could be,
yours,
to touch,
and kiss,
forever.

Centre Island Winter

A summery winter day,
The hourly skeleton ferry
Red, yellow, blue miniature toy tugs
Skyline shadows in the asphalt puddle.

Boardwalk and breakwater empty
Except the 15 second voice of the fog,
A bonfire smoke in the lake,
Then staring eyes of dead fish.

Man-made gardens and man-made
fountains
All sterile
Uniform sidewalks square by square,
Everything deadly civilized,
Nothing wild and fruitful.

Time, tea, and talk

With two fem friends,
Sitting in the kitchen,
Sipping the offered tea,
I look out the window
and watch the shadows
of once green trees
fade against the sunsetting sky……

But returning
to the conversation
we thrust and parry
about our physical features
and the other notions
of other peoples……

Till it's late,
and time to go,
with a laugh and bye
and bye,
maybe tomorrow.

Picnic Oasis

Shifting sands and gears,
A mirage! Of asphalt highway heat,
The navel of the desert,
The park of the city,
Over every dune, hill, more sand, more
cars.

A refuge and retreat,
A blade of grass in the white sugar,
A green patch in the grey,
Man-sown woods and gardens,
Painted benches and tables
Sterile walks to nowhere.

Unworthy, she kept her love

If she would cross a century
and release her pent passion
there would be no need
for this premature confession.

I suffer
at the crossroads of limbo,
the warm and the cool,
an ocean and continents,
deep in the love split,
for I have discovered her,
her very close friend.

What do I say
if she answers,
I've become tired
of my impotent charade
and now I aspire
to be your full-time lover
not your joe-boy brother?

There was no reply,
I'm nowhere and neither.

Carefree

Skip to the sidewalk,
Whistling the American Anthem,
Free for all smiles and hellos
Philosophical puns for fun generate groans.

Sing the way to Strawberry Fair,
Waving and weaving among the crowd.
Blow kisses to the fair ladies
Dodging the chestnut vendor's steam.

Merry dizzy ground twirls
Light cartwheeling floats

Then Subway line-up.

Candlemas

Lit for love,
playfully flaming,
flicker to, flicker fro,
colour changing,
candling flow,
liquid wick------splutter
to burn and melt
and drip into the holder.

Bad Samaritan

when beggars
break my stride
with their hands
and touch the mark
on my brow
I hate my shaking head

Holy Love Jamming Tie

On the perimeter of the party,
She sits on the balcony
With her hippy friend,
She strums and sings the songs
Of Donovan and Leonard Cohen,
In tune
Not clear and pure,
But her best
Steady and sure.

Passing the peace-pipe guitar
From cradle to cradle,
He sings his ready repertoire
With a hum and whistle,
That stills their souls to silence,
And they turn and look away into the night
Two hearts in harmony.

Through notes and voices,
There is a union
That soars and rejoices
A truly holy communion.

Transformation

poem on an envelope
rewritten and torn
wrong words and long lines
that are lost
in the creases and folds

changes form
on a
    clean
        white
           page

Rationalizing

black and white
square by square
change the rules
make contrary moves
strike, bold stroke
exile the king

it's only a game

The Unwilling Divorce

Back to work,
Watery widows eyes
On the bus
Thinking

Who cares?
Why can't he
Be here to see
The car light
Blinking?

Let time pass
Quickly,
365 bus rides
To it was a year ago
When.

Has to dream
Or lose his love and face
In the memory mist of
Time.

Should she change
The blacks
And perhaps marry
Again?

Who is he? the widow wonders.

Paying his dues

the mouthorgan man is
blowin' and a suckin'
to his cupped hands,
mumblin' those long ago
mean black memories,
playin' the blues low
in the cowboy washroom

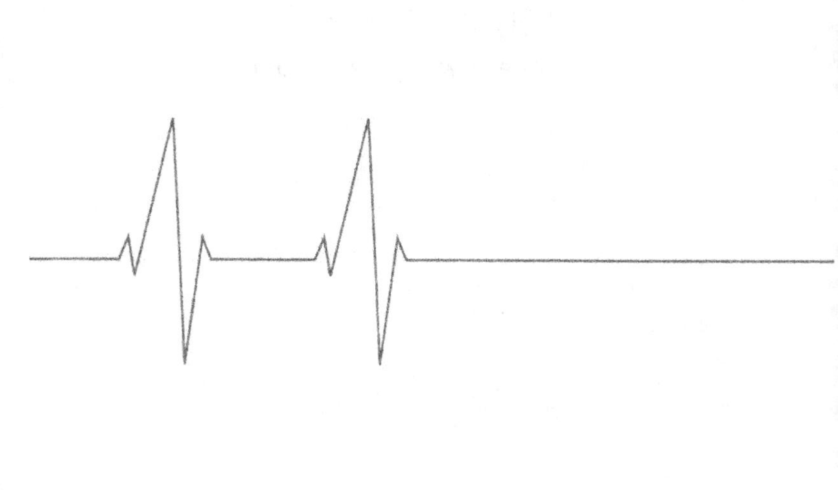

More than moth balls

In a bakery cake box
on the winter shoe rack
outside their sealed door
among the stale muffin crumbs
lies the sleeping ashes
of one of those
old overdosed ladies
I'm sure

and everything in between

After Loving Memories

The wind and the traffic
Rumble and roar on the street,
But in the cemetery
There is peace.

STONES OF THE TOMB
in loving memory of.

Some entered,
Some interred,
Monuments to soldiers
who died in the wars
who never knew.

FIGURINES
in loving memory of.

I walk by the rows
glancing at the dates.
Born and Died.
Some day some one
will pass my grave.
Born & Died.

PHALLIC SPIRES
in loving memory of.

There's a man
1846-1923.
He lived his life
without knowing me,
Yet many years later
I know of him.

TWO STOREY MAUSOLEUMS
In loving memory of.

The tombstone
and a few people's memories
are all that show
his existence.
And when they're gone
who knows?

Stop Moving the Furniture, God

Eyes wide awake.
And again.
Right over head.
And again.
Hide in my bed.

Try to rationalize,
If it hits you,
There is nothing
You can do,
But die.

I lay crouched
In a pre-natal pouch.

Just close my eyes,
And pray,
And wonder.
Is it moving away?
Are these my last thoughts?
Will I live to laugh
At my fears?

Count the seconds and years.
At last, it is over.
The lightning and thunder
Are miles away.

For the Sake of One Bite

But for one silly sinful apple
From the tree of right and wrong,
We would be naked in fields
Full of innocence and song.

A world-wide Garden of Eden
With no Land of Nod,
That Cherubim keep
For fugitive and vagabond.

A theme of love and peace
That allows and frees
A man to know,
And his woman to conceive,

In perfect pastures
Without worry of death
From war's murder,
The devil's disease
And swollen hunger.

But we can't blame,
Adam, or Eve his wife,
For we are all the same,
Taking fruit from the trees of life.

But for one silly sinful apple
In God's golden garden.

Christs Before The Comings

A thousand sandaled feet
clothed in pure and white linen
strut and glide in the street
waiting withdrawn and alone,

For their prophetic Elijahs
to begin the mission of their lives,

Or the end of kingdoms
at the doom of Revelation.

They wait,
for the star of Wormwood
and the waters to become blood.

They wait,
and there are pale horses
in their names.

The Witches' Floating Garden

At the far end
Of Wards Island
Where currents cross and circle
Round the cement wharves,
Along the hollow fathom channel,
In the harbour cove
Of black clasped mooring statues,
A pocket or glove
Of green mossweed water stews.

A jumping multitude of toads
Keep and care
Nature's haphazard horde,
The beachcomber's nightmare,
    A flotilla
Of twisted dead driftwood,
    A flotsam
Of pink legs of plastic dolls
And old rusted tin cans
And soft punk broken hulls.

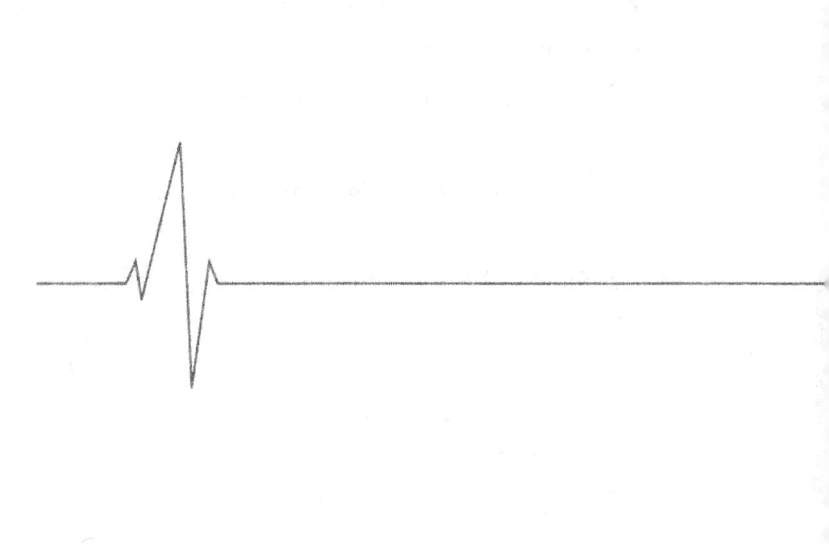

Torn Tickets and a Torn Man

An old man from Cabbage Town
and a misty system
strains and studies a chart
with a small pencil in his hand,
and shoulder-peering friends
disagree and agree
how to bet his money together
on their sure-fire
can't miss winner.

He placed his ten dollars
on the clean shiny counter
and received a ticket
for a horse
who was just
a machine name and number.

Rushing to the finish line,
he waits for the bugle,
parade and post-time.
He watches the odds on the tote,
and finally,
they're off on the chimes
and he returns home, broke.

Sand and Water Cathedral

All in sundry,
worshipping RA,
the golden round ball.

Fat,
dressed in black,
Italian women,
forever,
chasing their children
into the water.

Would-be gigolos,
curly hair, tan, and muscles,
prowl the beach,
ogling the girls,
who wear
brief and bulging
coloured underclothes.

Couples on towels
and sand,
wanting to make love,
but satisfying themselves
with holding hands
and rubbing on suntan oil.

Like to the God they pray,
to the sun they lay,
they are much the same
causing great pain
from the rod of God
and the burn of the sun.

The Never-Ever, Were-You-Ever Life

When you are young,
and you are supposed to have all this fun
of parties, girls and liquor,
but you put these off,
and wait for the future
and there is none,
and you're not.

When you are middle-aged,
and you're supposed to have
a wife, a house, and children,
and live on calendar marks
of due debts and claim checks,
and there is none,
and you're not.

When you are old
and you're supposed to have
rheumatism, wrinkles, and a pension,
and there's nothing in the past,
you look ahead to your last,
and there is none,
and you're not.

When were you ever,
anything at anytime.
You let your life out,
and wasted all your time.

You never were.

The fire

Somewhere along the way,
during the exchange of everyday
pleasantries and walking conversations,
I became aware of a catch in my breath
and a spark of affection in my breast
for you.

What started as a spark
through casual contact
has been fanned into a roaring fire
of love.
It's certainly not your fault
my appetite for your smile, your laugh,
and your presence has become voracious,
and I without thought have been selfish,
delighting in this exhilarating magic.

I understand your reluctance
and keeping your distance
from this raging fire that can burn
through our self-worth and perceptions,
never mind our unsullied reputations.

If you tell me you have no interest
or we can't take the risk,
then I must dampen the fire,
choke off the flame,
but you must know
there will always be hot embers
ready for you to stoke the fire
of my life-long love.

What may be

It's only you and me,
standing on the curb's edge,
waiting for the light to change,
and I can see
what may be
just down the road.

It's only you and me
working in our fruitful garden,
sharing lingering kisses
and long embraces
in our country haven,
side by side.

Please stay with me,
holding on to my dear-life hand
crossing this one way street,
so that many years from now,
neither one of us can say
only what might have been.

It's too late

It's too late
To withdraw from me now,
I'm caught
in your unintentional net of love.

There are no thoughts
of escape,
I see my self-danger
in devastation and depression.

Shall I tread water
until you're ready
to join me
or will you let me drown?

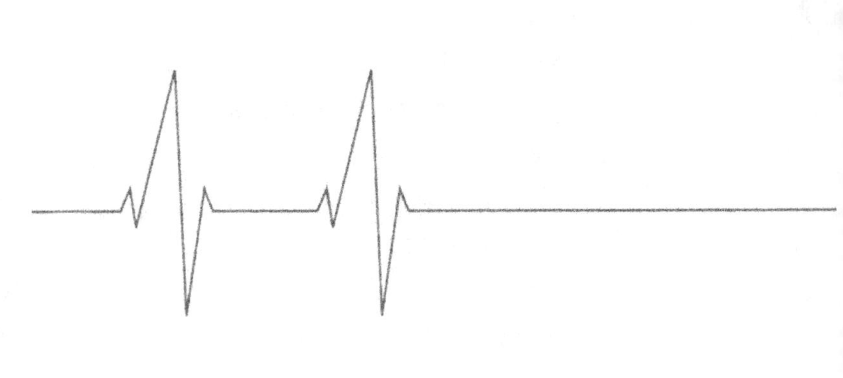

The secret life

Without you,
I went for a long walk,
not going anywhere in particular,
but as if I was being lead
I came to an abrupt stop,
in front of an open air book shop.

Without you,
I reached into the discount bin,
and discovered this discourse
on a secret life of plants,
and then coming to a realization,
I saw a parallel in our situation.

Without you,
I returned to our meeting place,
with my heart beating in my head
on having this exhilarating knowledge,
that we too could make space,
for a secret life without trace.

With you.

Circle of two

It doesn't matter
what others think,
it doesn't matter
what others say,
it doesn't matter
that they don't approve,
as long as we stay
in our circle of two,
round and round
circle of two.

As long as we're
face to face,
hand to hand,
lips to lips,
arm in arm,
and we're in love
in our circle of two,
round and round
circle of two.

It's our world,
it's our lives,
it's just you and me
in our love embrace,
and all we do
is just remain
unto ourselves
in our circle of two,
round and round
circle of two.

Departure Level

Seeing you off,
we couldn't overcome
your reserve.

My full measured
public embraces and kisses
were met
with perfunctory reluctance and resistance.

I was left
wondering
why won't you turn around
and wave goodbye?

Away

Yes, life goes on
but it's not the same,
my days,
full of measured emptiness,
end in nights
with my arm around your pillow
whispering your name,
---I miss you so.

3R's of loneliness

waitin'
for your return, is like
gettin' back to basics.
cause I pass the time
readin' ---- several books,
writin' ---- a few poems,
rithmetic ---- countin' the days.

Ready

Like the original pair,
with raised and open arms,
we spread our naked essence
on the shore of life.

Looking beyond horizon infinity,
together in love and alone,
exposed to the elements ----
of the wind and fire mores of society,
and running the gamut of emotions ----
of pain, joy, fear and ecstasy.

We will survive the storm.

Union Island

For all these years,
We have been travellers
            of the heart,
carrying our secrets
            and our dreams
too long,
out of sight, out of mind,
of friends and family
in our snap-open-close
luggage of love.

At long last,
Burning bridges, and beginning new lives,
we crossed the sea and the land,
you, by air
me, by land
to live openly together
on our union island
of love.

Island dreams

If dreams have colour,
then ours is yellow and gold,
rustling in the autumn wood
down along, a heritage road.

If dreams have sound,
then ours is a whisper and a roar
surging into a safe harbour
and over, a tranquil shore.

If dreams have a dimension,
then ours is eastern maritime
beating to an earlier time
across the gulf, of a common life line.

If dreams have a reality,
then ours is part way there
sharing our first time alone together
up the hill, from Hunter River.

Dead lover

Her new man
raised the subject,
and in explaining the status
of her previous lover,
she said,
"as far as I am concerned
he is dead."

He had his chance
and over time
he has ceased to exist.
"I'm not sending him
any card of greeting,
because the living
can't make contact
with the dead."

The discussion came to a close
on a jarring note
that the door remains open
to a dead lover,
as he can always
reach out to the living.

May he rest in peace.

Inclination 1

Dovetailed,
side by side
in our murphy bed lair,
I enfold your loveliness
with my bear body arms.

Inclination 2

Coiled,
we envelop each other
with intuitive understanding
and wordless wonder
at the love that flows between us.

free time

free time
comes to children
and
free time
comes to old men
free time
can be in a playground
free time
can be in a compound

the catch

casting an eye line
along the shore,
while trolling for beauty
in apparent ugliness,
and tacking to create sense out of chaos
in casual circumstances,
by fishing for found fragments
in wind and water whipped time,
and capturing and releasing graven images
in my mind's eye,
and at last,
landing framed visions
in a collage of life's debris.

at the changing of a light

sipping an early morning coffee at a
peaceful street patio
the maelstrom started with the faint
musical tinkling of a radio
at the changing of a light

a cacophony of voices, laughter, and horns
honking
pedestrians going in all directions bound
for the office
streetcars trundling through intersections
bells ringing
tourists peering and pointing at maps and
street signs
high overhead condominium construction
pounding
bicycle riders bopping in and out and
around traffic
urgent and impatient fire and ambulance
vehicles wailing

in the quiet sanctum of this whirlwind
driven crazy by a dream
drawn in by irresistible forces I follow the
same urban stream
at the changing of a light

before day breaks

standing by
deep in the darkness
of the hunkered building recess,
listening to
last night's debris
rustling in the breeze,
watching over
a homeless body
wrapped like a mummy,
I waited for the first arrival
as I heard the siren call
of a distant gull.

procrastinator

participating in a cause
when the objective
has been passed into laws

lobbying for a decision
when the vote
has already been taken

reaching out to a friend
who was moving away
to the south of New Zealand

mending broken fences
when the relationship
didn't make much sense

popping a marriage proposal
when the woman
is on her way to her nuptial

you missed all your opportunities
and now you are open
to deep and close scrutiny

the word

pity this poor poet's struggle
looking for the perfect word
to finalize a velvet verse,
stuck, racking my brain
thumbing thesaurus
clicking google
there's a word out there
somewhere
full of beauty and delight
succinct and precise
that expresses my feeling
and creates an understanding
of what I'm trying to convey

the wordsmith in me
is left wanting

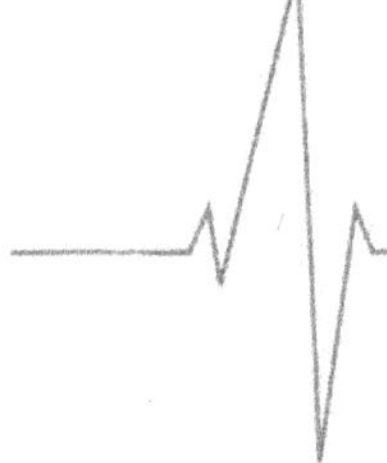

the luxury of being free

free
free as the proverbial bird
free of money concerns
free of routine
free of convention
free as Picasso
so free of commitment
you are alone
so free on the mountain
there's nowhere to go but down
free range
free verse
free hand
free love
free to be yourself
totally free
and then there is anarchy

advantages of agnosticism

why do we believe
what we believe
when it causes
war, death,
and unhappiness

we are born into this world
in all innocence
only to be corrupted
by wrong well-meaning agents

it's time
to purge yourself of faith,
to erase the implanted brainwash,
to ignore religious ridicule,
and to take no offense

bible and koran are no more
than fanciful fabrications
by people who lived
hundreds of years after
and thousands of years ago

cleanse yourself of evil evangelism
for there is no merit
to crusades and conversion
let us believe in ourselves

if human life is deemed precious
how can we allow it to be wasted
by flimsy pretexted reasons,
on the killing anvil
of a misguided mirage
of blasphemy and martyrdom

why do we believe
what we believe
when it causes
war, death,
and unhappiness

just a word

I thought I would reach out
in plenty of time
and make it more personal
by writing a letter in my own hand
but I have received nothing in return
I don't understand
surely out of courtesy
I thought you would respond

all it would take
is a few short words
to tell me definitively
where you stand

I know it's a hassle
to deal with postage
and possible paper cuts
and the awful taste of mucilage
and ink stains on your finger nails
but surely in this day and age
you could have sent me
an impersonal e-mail

all it would take
is a few short words
to tell me definitely
where you stand

I guess I can take it
from your callous silence
that you have deleted me
from your uncaring heart

out of order

in this landscape of desperation and
opulence
of have nots and have lots
stricken impoverishment versus excessive
affluence
one side wanting their fair share
the other vested protectors
of what they see is rightfully theirs
we have created an entrenched society
that lives behind gated communities
and in armed camps of plundering
marauders
who have turned to crime and anarchy
when they are life and death survivors
and there is no deterrent penalty
to stop these en masse pandemics
for which soldiers, police and security
are hands up helpless against
this kind of stone age blameless barbarity,
can we reverse the tipping point balance
of the scales of justice and economy?

putting pen to paper

it's been a long dreary afternoon
looking for some kind of inspiration
from listening
to the songs of Leonard Cohen

where will I find the spark?
one word that spawns
the writing of a poem

where will I find the idea?
looking at an abstract painting
or an interesting photograph

where will I find the intrigue?
watching the everyday activities
of people walking the streets

where will I find the mood?
as I sit in non-stoic isolation
while watching the snow swirl down

it's been a long cheery afternoon
looking for some kind of inspiration
and in the end
ironically I have written a poem

thank you Leonard

snubbed

I don't know what I said
I don't know what I did
what's with this aversion
of acknowledging my presence
we've been friends for years
and always part of the conversation

I know I don't run in the circles
of the current exalted company
but deliberately you've made me the
intruder
to this cozy group situation
for some reason I am being shunned
as the designated piranha
this last straw time round

I'll just go on
with my usual business
no reason to say goodbye
and that's why I just walked away
I guess I'm not worth
a little courtesy or the time of day

questions

is our conversation just a diversion?
whispers and sounds, smoke and mirrors
fresh-faced or covered in make-up
what does it mean?

what's really going on in the background?
sleight of hand, sleight of persona
beyond the curtain, behind the door
where's the key?

is our life like a game of chance?
risk-taker, love-maker
flipping cards or flipping pages
what's the end-game?

getting the message

I was only away
for a few scant days

the dog wasn't there
to greet me at the door

my hello echoed around
the stillness of the house

I climbed the stair
to find an unmade bed

your closet was empty
of all your clothes

I found a note on the table
with your final words

I stared out the window
and wondered
where you have gone
and thought
what do I do now

a plea to all would-be killers

there you stand
with gun in hand
cold and calculating
edgy and emotional
stop
hold fire
and look into their eyes
and see their humanity
with a family who will care and mourn
with a lover who will care and mourn
with friends who will care and mourn
with children who will care and mourn
how would you like to be the one
at the other end of the gun
they live, love, and breathe
just like you and me
what gives you the right
to end their life
is it really worth the killing

drifting down

he was at a loss
and out of a job
having left the house
just to go somewhere
a middle aged man
in a middle aged muddle
too young, too old
not old enough
no one returns his calls

hanging out in coffee shops
looking for stranger conversations
that don't ask
what are you doing now
the at first
giddy gleeful free time
is now leaden dead time
questions go unanswered
he just doesn't know

some call it a hobby

it's sad to see
you chasing celebrity

waiting throughout the day
to catch a glimpse
of some fleeting actor

who gives a wave
only to disappear
down some red carpet

it's sad to see
you calling out hysterically
please take a selfie with me

is your life so empty
of consequence
you feel the need
to join this butterfly dance

double sided

It all started
with the echo of my footsteps
down a long dark alleyway

I couldn't quite
put my finger on it

there were glimpses, traces, and flashes
of things that I had seen before
don't know when, don't know where

I couldn't quite
put my finger on it

a snatch of a familiar phrase recalled
a nostalgic pre-war song
in a time I didn't belong

I couldn't quite
put my finger on it

there was always something
just around the next corner
a shadow lurking in the mirror

I couldn't quite
put my finger on it

beyond the pale of life
there was another hand
behind the unseen curtain

I couldn't quite
put my finger on it

it all ended
on a boomy wooden bridge
with my crossing to the other side

watching women

laying in the long grass
out of my comfortable lair
a spent force
no longer in the hunt
eunuched by age
defanged and roarless
respected but no threat
just an old male animal
growling from the side lines
unseen on a mall bench

set aside

marginalized
on the side of the road
putting out my thumb to hitch a ride
never again
given due consideration
on the shore
watching life drift by
throwing out a line with a great hook
no longer in the mainstream
no ride no fish
no point in time
no catchhold

grim days

random human castaways
under ashen skies
forage and scavenge
in denuded forests,
and inundated shores,
and barren landscapes

ground zero

flashes from the future
phantoms from the past
looking ahead, looking behind
are those the members of the same cast?

what happened to the promises?
does it make any sense?
we keep travelling
but where are we going?
yesterday is tomorrow
tomorrow is today

I'm lost and found
despite sight and sound
I'm nowhere, somewhere, everywhere.

forever friends

growing up as friends from early years
carefree and casual
with walks to school and stories to tell
about sports, girls, and future glory

grown apart as friends in middle years
out of touch and out of mind
due to distances, families and careers
the bond still remained strong
as time moved along

grown together as friends in later years
unscathed by life's grind
we all have stories to tell
about sports, women and past glories

perspectives

I imagine taking the time
at some point in the future
sitting on an old wooden dock
with water lapping at my toes
watching ripple circles
from a fish breaking the surface
and listening for the echoes of loons
from across this back wooded bay

I imagine taking the time
at some point in the future
drifting in a worn out rowboat
with water spattering from the oars
watching hover circles
from a bird stalking the surface
and listening for the throes of doom
from across this dark wooded bay

I imagine taking the time
when currents and clouds intersect

clean slate

the old man didn't say it in so many words
on legs that were shakily unsteady
but make no mistake he was getting ready

he said, can you make use of it
as he opened the tool shed door
as I have no need of it anymore

he was busily divesting himself of worldly
goods
to lessen his children's bored burden
of sorting through his life's accumulation

he was cleansing himself of collected
clutter
migrating from the materialistic world
through the eye of the needle spiritual
world

out of respect and understanding
of his need to give it away
we were honour bound to take it away

something more than lament

in our younger days
it never crosses our minds
in our older days,
it never leaves our minds

it has always happened to others
your second cousin removed
a friend of a friend's mother
someone else always shows up dead

do I have much of a future
how long have I to survive
what date on the calendar
will I be meeting my demise

notables

it falls to the few
by break ins, break outs, and
breakthroughs
firsts and lasts and bests
triumphs and failures
unique and antique characters
who make a real difference
by touching the lives of people
around us and beyond us

on a pinnacle

battered and bullied
by all the questions
and the barrage
of options
in making decisions
I'm inching to the edge

the pulse of life keeps pumping
as I dither to and fro on jumping

wracked by doubt and procrastination
and wringing my hands in frustration

no longer can I play the man in waiting
to see what way the wind is blowing

right or wrong
up or down
right or left
east or west
north or south
with or without

keeping my own company
I will come to an epiphany

disavowal plea

I may not appear today
as you saw me yesterday

I haven't always been
as you think I am

you will not find me
as you found me before

you will not know me
as you knew me before

you can't count on me
as you counted on me before

please embrace
whoever you think I am

what time is it?

wall street time or island time
I'm with the enlightened Einstein
on the relativity of time
I haven't found any shifting paradigm
on the question of time
I'm all for the sublime
of going beyond conventional time
I will be the eager enzyme
on my own physical capsule of time
I'm using this final defusal rhyme
on the bomb of my ticking time

what time is it?

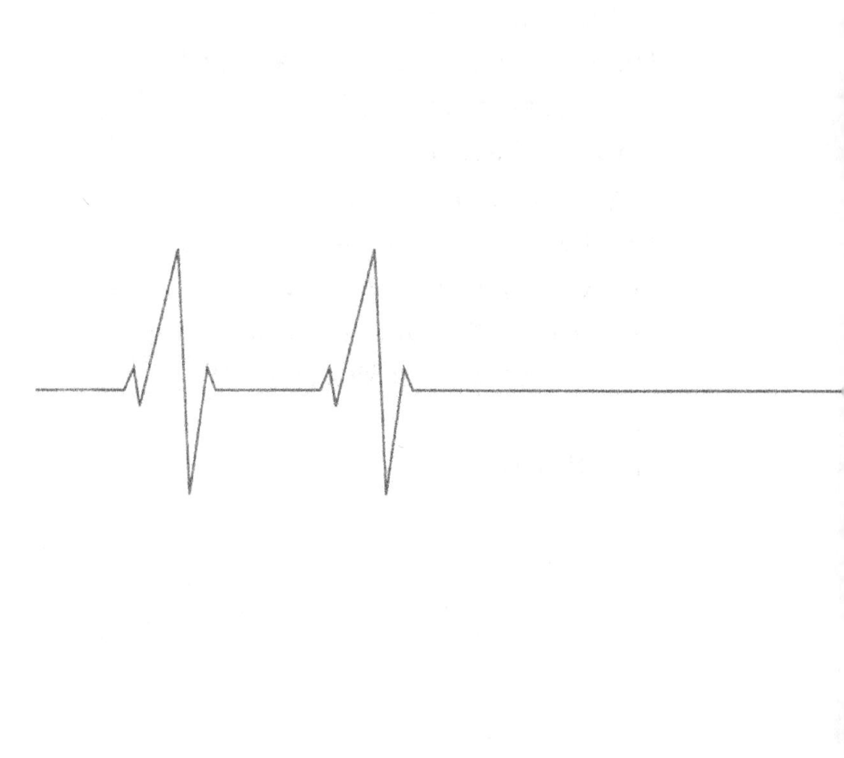

a mask has slipped

the persona façade
has started to crumble

the fault lines
are beginning to show

will you accept
my many alter egos

will you accept
my appeasing placebos

what has been internalized
is now externalized

the domesticated beast
is dead

who is he anymore

is he the boy
who cried
when his mom
took him to kindergarten

is he the actor
who played
Irwin Ingham
in the struggles of Little Malcolm

is he the husband
who separated
from his wife and children
and found another woman

is he the politician
who knocked
at voters' doors
asking for their support

is he the farmer
who harvested
flowers and garlic
and sold them at market

is he the photographer
who snapped
the medusa brainstorm
on New Zealand shores

is he the poet
who wrote
the finality of it all
in the corner of the upstairs hall

is he the old man
who growled
at his reflection
and lack of recognition

who am I anymore

mournful1

now that you are gone
I am hollow and alone
silence so deep
I am listening
to the house creak
I am listening
to the kitchen tap drip
I am listening
to the pound of pulse ring
in my ears

mournful2

down the dark hole
of loneliness
do I sense another presence
sitting at the table
watching the traffic roll by
once part of the stream
now just a daydream

mournful 3

standing by the stair
unmoving
awash in despair
everyday much the same
no one to really care
in this holding pattern
waiting for the end
where do I go from here

enjoy the moment

there is no lasting legacy
we are here and we are gone
in the great scheme of things
what did it all mean
eons after the great implosion
the world keeps turning
as a microcosm of space
the winds of desolation
sweep this cold denuded world
nothing is left but the remnants
from this bygone civilization
just like the myths of Atlantis
a society that rushed
to its own extinction
everything we stood for
is for naught
all that we do is so temporary,
enjoy the moment

old options

sifting through the strands
of old dramas
going over well worked grounds
listening to the dialogue
of past conversations in my head
what if I had changed my mind
what if I hadn't said what I said
things might have been different
can't help but enflame fervent feelings
by repeating it over and over again
it never really leaves me
it's always there
running through scenes
where I make an appearance
it's not so much a regret
but a wistful debt
to something long gone

ready or not

getting ready
for the deep cold of winter
tidying up loose ends
putting away summer's debris
shutter some of the windows
sun sinking lower in the sky
the darkness spreads

it will inevitably come!
will I see the light of spring again?
the garlic is in the ground!
am I going to part of the winter kill?
the farmers' market starts up in May!
will I need my last word and will?
I'm not ready!!!

quest

searching for the individuality
the flower among the weeds

searching for the clarity
the door through the fog

searching for the purity
the seed among the chaff

searching for the fantasy
the lost love on the internet

searching for the authenticity
the Holy Chalice or the Holy Grail

searching for the certainty
the treasure of Oak Island

searching for the epiphany
the idea among the tweets

searching for the essentiality
the word on the page

the ongoing quest continues.....

looking for Jane Manning

I was so beguilingly distracted
by your casual sensuality
I can't remember what you taught

I still see you with dark hair
in a tight French roll
sitting on a desk in a short mini-skirt

you always made an impression
with your winsome smile
these are images a young man doesn't
forget

I made some double-entendre remark in
class
and you called me a dirty old man
but we understood each other flirt to flirt

you teased all the testosterone-driven guys
and you knew only too well
the playfully intended cause and effect

you're probably long retired and off the grid
you could be almost anywhere
in the south of France or in East Newport

Jane, you've gone missing, are you still with
us?

nothing but time

as a young boy on the porch step
on a hot early August day
with friends away at the cottage
time moves slowly
waiting for our school to start

as an old man on the porch step
on a hot early August day
with friends already in storage
time moves quickly
waiting for a roll call to depart

mourn the loss

the words stops at mid-phrase
the music stops on a hanging note
the painting stops on a fading brush stroke

the pen
the guitar
the palette
drop to the floor

we scramble
for pre-published manuscripts
for missing track recordings
for unfinished canvasses

anything to revive
the writer
the musician
the artist

gone

with these words
I am reaching out and reaching back
grasping at the threads of my life
picturing people as I remember them
wondering whether our paths were meant
to be crossed once
and never to be crossed again

they meant something to me then
and I'm sure I meant something to them

the tie that connected us was loosened
and we just drifted further and further apart
without ever giving it another thought

they have gone missing never to return
where are they now?
how did I get here?

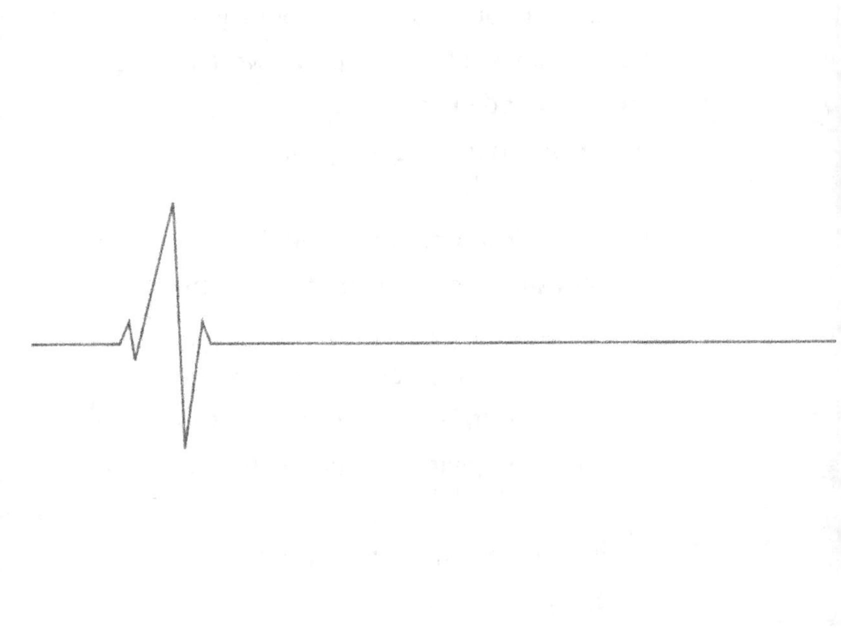

the finality of it all

maybe, it's the gravity of the occasion,
as the followers of funerals
swirl around the periphery,
I'm trying to conjure up some kind of
distraction

maybe, it's the lowering of the coffin,
as the grievers at the grave
bow their heads in sanctity,
I'm trying to conjure up some kind of
distraction

maybe, it's the covering of the coffin,
as the family shovels earth
on the last vestiges of reality,
I'm trying to conjure up some kind of
distraction

maybe, it's the final life procession,
as the gathered disassemble
one by one from the cemetery,
I'm trying to conjure up some kind of
distraction

maybe, it's why I ask this question,
will I cry at my own funeral?

ephemerals

leaving behind

something more than
skid marks on a road

something more than
a lesson on a chalkboard

something more than
sand castles on the shore

something more than
whispers behind a closed door

something more than
footprints in the snow

something more than
a head crater on a pillow

something more than
sight-seeing from a mountain outlook

something more than
scribbling words in a note book

something more than
a blip on traffic radar

something more than
an obit in the newspaper

something more than

____

where is my stonehenge?

lives spent

what more can be said
we have spent our lives

making the most use
of what we have been given

chasing the moving target
of the unobtainable and unfathomable

looking for the perfect essence
of eden and nirvana

trying to give our existence
some ultimate meaning

hoping to leave behind
some kind of lasting legacy

seeking serenity and acceptance
that really comes only with death

what more can be said
we have spent our lives

endgame

others have left before me
others will leave after me
my game's end is not what I expected
but it is the end I have been dealt

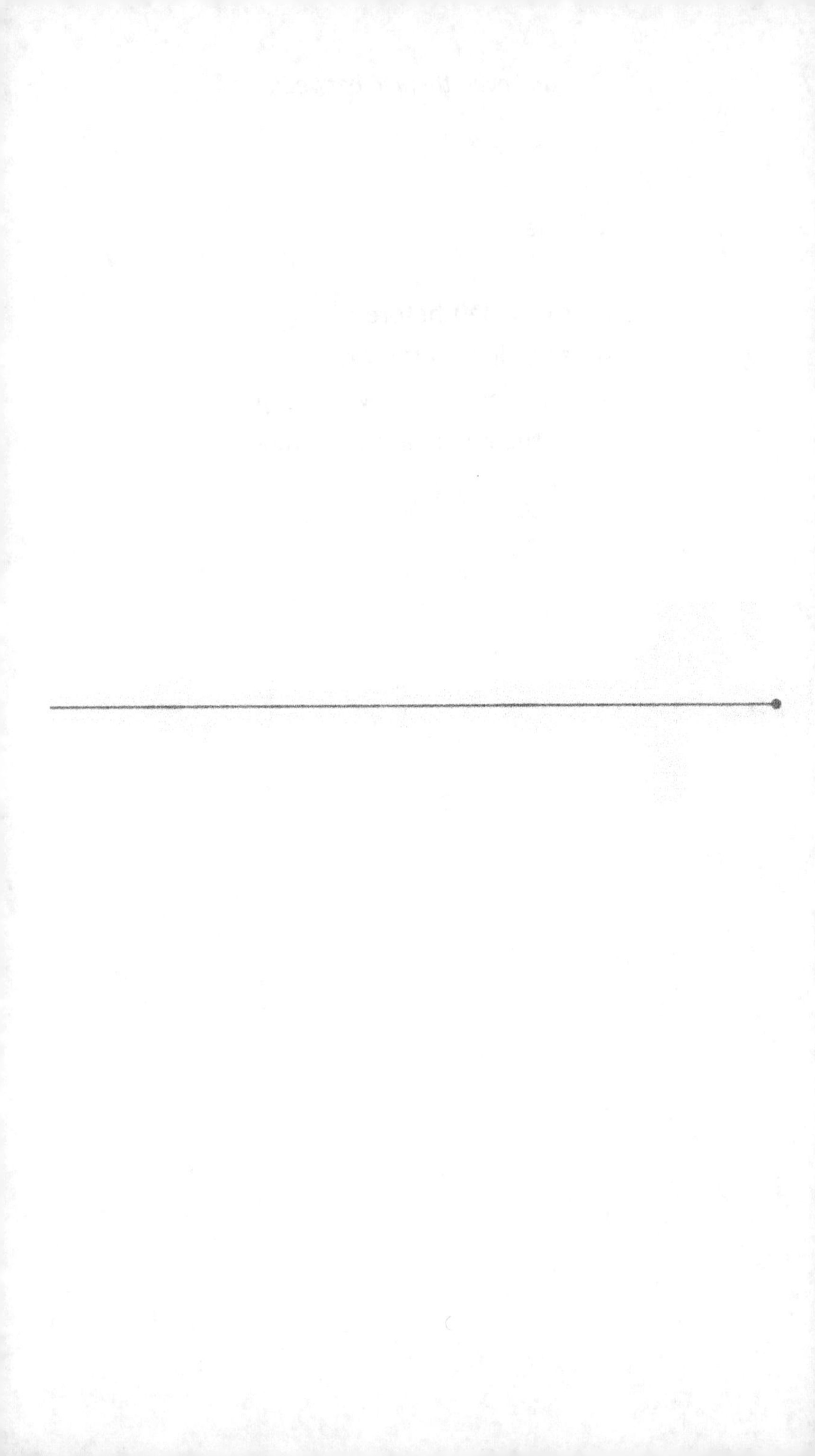

– exit light